IMAGES
of America

BRIDGEWATER

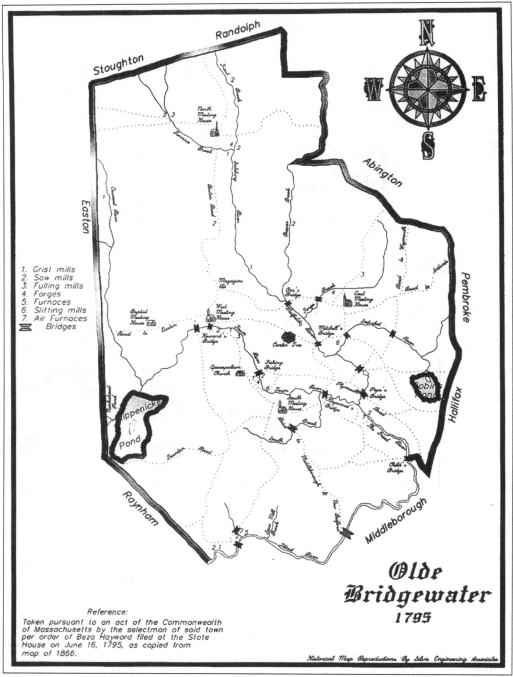

Shown here is the town of Bridgewater in 1795 before it was broken up into the four towns of Bridgewater, East Bridgewater, West Bridgewater, and Brockton. By this time, the six-mile circle had already been carved to this configuration.

2

IMAGES
of America

BRIDGEWATER

David R. Moore

ARCADIA
PUBLISHING

Published by Arcadia Publishing
Charleston, South Carolina

Library of Congress Catalog Card Number: 2003110237

For all general information, contact Arcadia Publishing:
Telephone 843-853-2070
Fax 843-853-0044
E-mail sales@arcadiapublishing.com
For customer service and orders:
Toll-free 1-888-313-2665

Visit us on the Internet at www.arcadiapublishing.com.

CONTENTS

ACKNOWLEDGMENTS

More than 15 years ago, a small group of Bridgewater residents—Mike Bois, Ruth Bishop, and Dorothy Mann—met to share their recollections on Bridgewater postcards. The group decided that it might be fun to reproduce them and other Bridgewater photographs for others to enjoy. Jim Buckley and Ken Moore, who had volunteered their time to open the Bridgewater Public Library Historical Room, also found that there was need to make Bridgewater history more accessible. These two groups, along with Arthur Lord and Bobby Copeland, organized under the name of the Bridgewater Collectors and began to assemble materials for publication.

From their efforts arose four books: *Bridgewater Illustrated, Tales around the Common, Cranes History*, and *A Pictorial History*. These books made available many photographs and stories that would have been otherwise lost in time. It is our hope that this book will once again make those pictures available for enjoyment by those who share a love of history. We also hope that it will foster an interest in the history of the town and help us further preserve the area of greatest need, the 20th century.

I would like to acknowledge the original efforts of the Bridgewater Collectors, as well as George Rizer and the Lions Club, the Bridgewater Historical Commission, Ben Spence, and many other members of the community for their contributions to this book.

—David R. Moore, Chairman
Bridgewater Historical Commission

INTRODUCTION

Bridgewater, a town in southeastern Massachusetts, started much the same as many of the early colonies. Inhabitants of the Plymouth Colony soon realized that their rapidly growing settlement would need more farmland to provide sustenance. Exploration had shown that the land 20 miles to the west on the southeastern corner of the great swamp filled their needs. A river would provide transport to the coast and waterpower for mills. The land was reasonably flat and the soils were fertile, unlike the sandy soils of the Plymouth Colony.

Negotiations, begun in 1640 with the Native Americans, gave the colonists the ownership to a six-mile radius circle of land in 1656. The name chosen for the first inland settlement of the Plymouth Colony was Bridgewater. The king gave grants to a group of men from Duxbury for parcels that consisted of approximately 40 to 50 acres bordering the Town River, the lifeblood of the settlement. Only a few of these men would ever actually settle on those parcels; many were given to children or sold off. The geographic center of the village was the "center tree." Today, a granite post near the intersection of the Old Colony rail line and Route 106 marks the location of that tree. The earliest meetinghouse was on the site of the church in West Bridgewater, and the colony grew from there to form the towns we know today as West and East Bridgewater, the city of Brockton, and our Bridgewater.

In 1712, citizens of the southern section of town petitioned the church to form the South Parish, for a sufficient number of settlers now lived in the area to support their own church. For the next 70 years, the town was little more than a farming community with a small center built around the crossroads of Main Street, South Street, and Summer Street, on the hill just above the river. A number of small mills sprang up in town, creating Carver's, Blood, Skeeter Mill, and Sturtevant's Ponds for waterpower. The Town River was also dammed in two locations, at High Street and Plymouth Street, but these early industries were closely controlled by the English government and limited to serving the needs of the Crown.

It would not be until after the American Revolution that our small town would blossom into what we know today as Bridgewater. The mills "hit the ground running" at the close of the revolution. The Perkins ironworks on High Street became a leading producer of iron plate for nails, shovels, and eventually boilers and heavy castings. The paper mill on Plymouth Street was the first in the colony. The Keith foundry, at Sturtevant's Pond, and the Washburn foundry, at Carver's Pond, supplied local iron. A few shipyards were also located along the river, producing craft larger than the *Mayflower*.

In town, the "age of enlightenment" began in 1760, when Reverend Sanger and Reverend Shaw organized their Greek and Latin Academy. In 1799, the Bridgewater Academy opened, and in 1840, the Bridgewater Normal School was founded. The number of churches increased in 1850 with the opening of the Trinity Congregational in Scotland, the Roman Catholic, and (in the town center) the New Swedenborgian and Methodist.

The railroad brought on the second expansion in town along with the industrial revolution. The days of Bridgewater as an agricultural community were numbered.

The second half of the 19th century was one of factories, manufacturing, and immigrant labor that would forever add color to the character of the community. The workers, who initially came from the cities by rail and streetcar to work in the factories along the tracks, found a new home. The Irish and Italians in the Stanley section, and the eastern Europeans on the east side of the tracks, would challenge and eventually comingle with the conservative New England Yankee ruling fathers.

Today, Bridgewater has once again been transformed by its residents. Many have found work outside of the community by the benefit of Route 24, Interstate 495, and the commuter rail line. Other than those who work at the prison, college, or in the town, we have become a bedroom community.

The pictures in this book, reprinted by the Lions Club, are just a few of those that show the past in our town. Each brief description could be a thousand words or more. The Bridgewater Historical Commission and the Bridgewater Historical Collectors have accumulated a large collection, which is stored in the Bridgewater Public Library Historical Room and in storage facilities donated by Consolidated Recycling and Spartago Masonry. It is our hope that someday we will have a place of our own, so that someday all can enjoy and learn from the past.

For now we hope that this book will foster an interest in our beautiful town and encourage you to document your history for the future.

One

INDUSTRY

The most famous and longest-running industry in Bridgewater was the ironworks on High Street at the Town River. In 1695, Robert Perkins was granted permission to dam the river and flood a reservoir of approximately 400 acres. From this early mill would grow an industry spanning almost three centuries. By 1863, the Lazell Perkins Iron Company had become the second-largest iron rolling and forging mill in the country. The iron timbers used to construct the pilothouse on the USS *Monitor* were cast and forged by men at the plant.

Looking down High Street toward the Bridgewater Iron Works plant *c.* 1890, one could see about 30 buildings of the once great iron-manufacturing complex that lined the river valley. Although the plant started sometime after 1695, it would not thrive until the arrival of the railroad in 1845. The railroad, however, would also bring its demise with the consolidation and relocation of the country's iron-manufacturing centers to the West in the 1880s.

Tim Madden stands next to his team of oxen at Stanley Iron Works among piles of pig iron *c.* 1915. The plant specialized in making iron plate and other parts for Stanley factories in New Britain, Connecticut. When it closed in 1928, a number of Bridgewater families moved to Connecticut to stay with the company.

The Bridgewater Iron Company had a large display at the Philadelphia Centennial Exposition in 1876. During the Civil War, it was the second-largest iron-rolling plant in the country. It produced large amounts of boilerplate for the locomotive shops in Taunton and the rest of New England.

This *c.* 1880 photograph depicts the Perkins foundry as seen from the roof of the Eagle Cotton Gin Company, at the foot of Pearl Street. In 1848, a fire destroyed the foundry section. Henry Perkins, who was running that section, opened his own plant just across the railroad tracks on Broad Street. Men returning from the Civil War in 1865 were employed to construct a new building that would serve as the main furnace area for the plant until 1974. The plant operated for more than 150 years in the same family, producing quality iron castings of all sorts, including nail machinery and piano backboards.

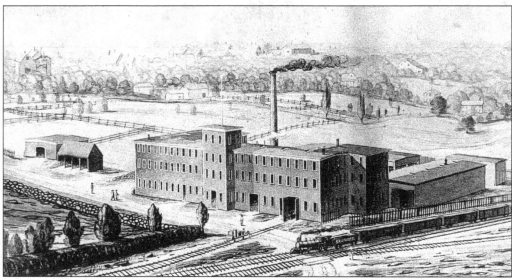

The Eagle Cotton Gin Company evolved from Hyde, located at the head of Bedford Street. This new plant, built by Hyde, was located at the base of Pearl Street, next to the railroad. The company merged with the Continental Cotton Gin Company in 1899 and continued to operate until the late 1920s at the same location.

The Eagle Cotton Gin Company ran under the direction of the Bates and Hyde Cotton Gin Company until it consolidated with the Continental Cotton Gin in 1899. About half of the buildings seen here were demolished after 1915, and the remaining structures were used as a lumberyard for many years.

A cotton gin is a machine that separates the cotton fibers from the seed hulls at a rate 500 times faster than hand labor. These machines, made in Bridgewater by Eagle (seen here), Bates and Hyde, Carver, and Continental, were sold all over the world from the 1820s on and revolutionized the cotton industry. They also made slavery much more profitable for the plantation owners.

The L. Q. White Shoe Factory, Bridgewater, Mass.

A common practice was for shoe manufacturers to solicit public financial support to raise capital for the opening of a shoe plant. This was done for McElwain, L.Q. White, and J.E. Lucey by issuing bonds or shares in the company. The largest shoe company ever to operate in Bridgewater was L.Q. White, starting in 1909. The company produced large orders of army shoes for foreign countries such as Belgium and Russia. Production during World War I may have exceeded 24,000 shoes per day. During the 1920s, L.Q. White employed more than 5,000 employees and produced 450 dozen pair of shoes a day in the main plant on Spring Street and the former McElwain plant on Perkins Avenue. The plant was closed in 1933 due to labor problems.

The L. Q. White Shoe Factory, Bridgewater, Mass.

This view from Spring Street shows the L.Q. White plant *c.* 1930 at the height of its production.

Following the sudden closure of the L.Q. White plant in 1935, the George O. Jenkins Company used the complex for the storage of leather and paper scrap. In 1942, the rear, five-story brick portion of the plant was destroyed by fire. The burned section of the structure remained until 1959, when the rest of the building, then filled with chickens, burned.

After the fire in 1942, the burned-out rear section of the L.Q. White building stood for almost 20 years alongside the tracks. The remainder of the building burned c. 1960.

The McElwain Shoe Company was the town's most important shoe firm in 1910. The firm was famous for keeping workers employed year-round in an otherwise seasonal business. It was also known for the $2 shoe. The new plant on Perkins Street was opened in 1898 through public subscription under the leadership of treasurer Samuel P. Gates. The plant closed in 1915 following a one-year labor action. The majority of McElwain's production moved to other McElwain plants in Manchester, New Hampshire.

William McElwain's first factory was on Hale Street in 1894, near the railroad. It buned down and wasy replaced in 1898 by the present building on Perkin's Avenue. William H. McElwain lived from 1867 to 1908.

People work inside the modern W.F. McElwain plant *c.* 1900. Seventy-five percent of the wall area was windows to provide natural lighting for the workers. This scene—except for electric lights—would be very similar to what appeared 75 years later.

The labor force at McElwain was made up of mostly immigrants. Local workers, seen here *c.* 1900, caused turmoil in 1096 when strikebreakers arrived from the other McElwain plant in Manchester, New Hampshire, as reported by the *Bridgewater Independent*.

The McElwain building was later reopened as the George Jones Shoe Company, and later still as L.Q. White. In 1938, Bridgewater citizens helped John E. Lucy from Middleboro open a plant, which operated until the 1970s. George E. Keith and Walkover Shoe of Brockton ran the plant until its final closing in 1994.

George O. Jenkins turned the paper mill into one that manufactured a leather-like cardboard material for cheaper shoes. It was later taken over by Hooker and Warren, then the Hollingsworth family of Milton, who ran it from 1857 to 1896. Hiram and George O. Jenkins purchased the plant in 1896 and made a leather substitute until the late 1970s, at this site and also upriver at the No. 2 plant on High Street. The Plymouth Street mill (seen here in 1935) closed in 1972, and the High Street plant in 1980.

The fire at the Jenkins' mill leveled the plant in August of 1908. It was rebuilt with new machinery. Part of the modernization was to purchase a motor truck to aid in the delivery of product to the area shoe factories.

The Over Globe Shoe Company was one of the many businesses to later occupy the early Carver Cotton Company buildings on Spring Street. The advent of the McKay stitching machine and abundant immigrant labor was a boon to the shoe industry in Bridgewater. Many of the shoe businesses in town started in the old fairgrounds building on Broad Street, which was torn down in 1944.

Seen here is the final shoe company to occupy the Carver building on the west end of Spring Street. Just prior to World War I, a group of Bridgewater citizens of eastern European heritage banded together to form the Bridgewater Workers Cooperative, or "the Coop," to manufacture shoes. During that time, the building added upper floors and connected the buildings before it also closed in 1988.

In 1900, three local men—Walter S. Little, J. Gardner Bassett, and Hosia Kingman—began the Eastern Grain Company at the intersection of Plymouth Street and the railroad. In 1902, Little took over complete ownership of the plant. He was forced to rebuild in 1910 following a devastating fire. Over the years, under his leadership, Eastern Grain grew to a large concern. One of his popular methods of operation was to supply the chickens and grain to farmers and then pay for the chicken at the time of market. In 1936, Little sold out to Corn Products International, who continued to bag grain at that location until 1975. Flora Little, his wife, was a great benefactor of the town, contributing large amounts of money to the Bridgewater Improvement Association and the Bridgewater Public Library.

Agway took over the Eastern Grain operation in 1975 and eventually moved the retail sales to another location on Spring Street. In 1978, the abandoned plant, which was the tallest building ever erected in Bridgewater, burned down.

The Bridgewater Water Company built the waterworks in 1887 on Sprague's Hill on the corner of High and Broad Streets, an ideal site since, at 185 feet, it is the highest point in Bridgewater. This private company owned and managed the water system, which supplied Bridgewater and East Bridgewater. The works remained in private hands until the devastating fires at the college and in the town center in 1924, which proved the system inadequate for major fire protection. In 1925, the waterworks became a public utility, and the Board of Water Commissioners was created.

Two

CHURCHES

This early drawing depicts the second South Parish Meeting House in 1800. The original meetinghouse was dedicated in 1717. This building, built in 1760, was modified over the years before being taken down in 1845. According to the epitaphs of Old Bridgewater, the cemetery did not have engraved stone markers until sometime well after its establishment in the early 1700s. The site later housed the Unitarian church.

The "First Cemetery 1716" is one of the most historic and aesthetic settings in Bridgewater. Located on the corner of Summer and Plymouth Streets, this burial ground, now tree-shaded and surrounded by a low rubble stone wall, is part of the two acres that John and Rebecca Washburn deeded to the newly created South Parish for the building of the first meetinghouse. It was the sole cemetery of the South Parish until *c.* 1750 and continued to be an important burial ground until the 1840s, when the new cemetery on Mount Prospect Street was established. The graves of many "soldiers, sailors, and Patriots" of the American Revolution are found in this burial ground, the second-oldest historical feature in Bridgewater's center, predated only by the slightly older Tory House in Central Square.

Shown here is the First Church on School Street as it appeared for 60 years. Land on the front lawn was then sold to the state for construction of the college gymnasium.

The Unitarian church was erected on the site of the first meetinghouse in the South Parish in 1846. The Christopher Wren steeple contained a bell cast in Paul Revere's foundry in Canton. A hurricane in 1954 lifted the spire and dropped it through the roof. The bell was then sold to a man in California to help cover the cost of reconstruction. During renovation work in the 1980s, a trompe l'oeil style of wall decoration was discovered under many layers of paint and was beautifully restored.

The present Trinity Episcopal Church, at the corner of Main and Pearl Streets, was consecrated in 1884. It has the distinction of being one of the two Bridgewater churches that traces its origins back to the 18th century.

The Episcopal church, seen here in 1880, was located on the upper end of Main Street next to the cemetery. This second structure, erected in 1836, replaced one that had stood for many years across the street. Records state that the first building was still used beyond its time, open to the weather with no windows.

Construction of St. Thomas Aquinas Church began in the 1850s. The earliest photograph of shows a small belfry on the front. The church was originally run from the Hibernia Society Hall, at 42 Center Street. Irish Catholic families that constituted the neighborhood in the area of the ironworks were instrumental in bringing the religion to town.

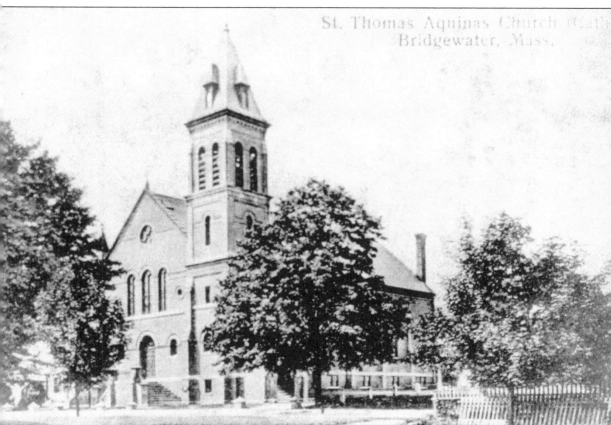
St. Thomas Aquinas Church (Cath.)
Bridgewater, Mass.

Early attempts of the Irish Catholic community to construct a structure out of wood supposedly failed because of mysterious fires in the dark of night. The final structure, the first St. Thomas Aquinas Church, had only four windows along the side. A later addition added two more and a beautiful bell tower to the front. The Catholic church is pictured here with the bell tower, following the second major addition to the structure. A move to construct another Catholic church occurred c. 1900 to serve the needs of a small French Canadian population in town. Land was purchased and a foundation begun on the end of Standish Avenue before the archdiocese intervened and brought the French Canadians back into St. Thomas.

This home, located at 36 Main Street, was used as the meeting place for a Catholic service for French immigrants in the area. The other Catholic church in town, St. Thomas Aquinas (on Center Street), eventually brought them into its service with the aid of a French priest sent from Boston. Just prior to this time, c. 1900, the French immigrants had begun building their own church, the New French Parish, at the end of Standish Avenue behind the house. That foundation stood until 2002.

The Scotland Trinitarian Congregational Church was erected in 1822 as a place of worship for a group of parishioners who had left the First Parish in protest over its increasingly Unitarian nature. While it is the third-oldest church organization in Bridgewater, it occupies the oldest church building still extant in town. Located on the corner of Pleasant and Prospect Streets, this church has been labeled one of the finest Federal-style meetinghouses in southeastern Massachusetts.

Soon after the establishment of the Congregational church in Scotland, many Bridgewater residents felt the need to have a new, larger church on the town common. Central Square Congregational Church was erected on the corner of Church Street and Central Square in 1836. The church burned in 1860, and this slightly larger structure was rebuilt on the same location. In 1956, an addition was placed on the rear of the church to accommodate a growing population. In 1959, the steeple was struck by lightning and replaced by a smaller spire with the clock in the base of the tower.

The First Baptist Church, on Summer Street, was dedicated on March 5, 1902. The church was formally organized in 1897 and held its services in the newly erected Odd Fellows Hall on Central Square until the present church building was completed. Although this parish has never had a large membership, it has been active in the community during its 100 years, providing, among other things, a gymnasium in 1916, a servicemen's center in World War II, and a drop-in center for the elderly in 1973.

This simple meetinghouse on Cedar Street holds an important place in the history of Bridgewater. Built in 1834 to house the congregation of the New Jerusalem Church, it was the first church building of the Swedenborgian faith to be erected in New England. In addition, it is the second-oldest church structure in town, passed only in age by the Scotland church. This building would later house Methodists in the 1870s, following the construction of the new Swedenborgian structure on the corner of School and Bedford Streets.

The present New Jerusalem Church, in the southeast corner of the town center, was built in 1871 on the site of the first town hall. Joseph A. Hyde, a member of the church and owner of the Bates and Hyde Cotton Gin Company, which owned the factory and most of the land at the head of Bedford Street, was a very generous benefactor of the church. He was instrumental in the construction of this beautiful new church at the south end of the common in 1871. The building was heavily damaged by fire in 1996 but was rebuilt to near its original condition with the help of the community.

Three

TRANSPORTATION

The first railroad station in Bridgewater, at Broad Street, was built of wood in 1847. It sat closer to Broad Street than the existing one. The patch on the roof was a repair from a fire caused by sparks from an engine or coal stove, a very common problem along the rail line.

Looking south down the tracks at Broad Street *c.* 1890, you would have seen two sets of tracks and two stations. A freight station can be seen on the left, with the crossing tenders shack on the right. In the distance just past the original station can be seen the spout from the water tower for filling the engines.

Bowman's Express was located next to the hotel on Central Square at the head of Summer Street. The company worked with the railroad to deliver goods throughout the town.

Each of the seven crossings in town had a small building or station that was tended by a guard or gatekeeper. Flagg Street Station may have been a little bigger to serve the needs of the Gammons Sawmill, located in the field southwest of the crossing, where the soccer field parking lot is today.

South Bridgewater Station was located just north of the Titicut Street railroad crossing and served the needs of the state farm and North Middleboro.

Situated northwest of the Wall Street railroad crossing, Stanley Station served the needs of the ironworks neighborhood. The second floor was used as an apartment.

A new railroad station was erected in 1893 on Broad Street just south of the old station, which had been built in the 1840s, when the railroad first came to Bridgewater. This new depot, a rock-faced granite structure, accommodated rail passengers until 1959. When commuter rail service reopened in 1995, insufficient parking in the area forced the stop to move a half-mile south to the Bridgewater State College campus.

Two sets of tracks, first opened in 1845, ran south through Bridgewater to Middleboro. The Old Colony Railroad originally started in Fall River and was later completed to Boston. The railroad was the catalyst for industry in town, as it connected the factories to the seaports along the coast, bringing in raw materials and labor. Passenger service ended in 1959. Commuter rail service from Boston to Middleboro resumed in 1995.

This *c.* 1920 photograph shows the new Bridgewater railroad station, as seen from Broad Street. The water tower in the background is part of L.Q. White's shoe factory. Following the end of commuter rail service in 1959, the station sat empty for many years before being purchased by Walkover Shoe, on Perkins Avenue, for storage, sales, and parking. After the factory closed in 1994, the space was reopened as a restaurant.

Tinkam's Corner was located at the corner of Prospect and Pleasant Streets in Scotland. Probably built in the mid-1800s, it did not get it's name until 1905, when it was purchased by Mr. Tinkam. It served the needs of the neighborhood as a general store but was later limited to a neighborhood grocery. It was converted to professional shops in the late 1970s.

38

William Bassett opened a Ford dealership c. 1910 at the beginning of Main Street, selling cars and tractors. He eventually changed to Pontiac and Cadillac before closing in the 1950s. The building was used for a few years as a furniture factory before being taken down for a new retail store.

When electric streetcars made their debut in Bridgewater in 1897, this form of public transformation was in its second decade of phenomenal expansion throughout the nation. The laying of the tracks, the building of the power plants, and the stringing of the electric wires were duly noted by Bridgewater citizens. By 1900, they routinely traveled by trolley to Taunton, Middleboro, Brockton, and East Bridgewater, and by making connections, to other cities like Providence, Rhode Island. For 30 years, the trolleys served the citizens of the town.

Shown here is one of the electric streetcars that ran along Broad Street to Elmwood and East Bridgewater. Service from Bridgewater Center was interrupted by the railroad tracks. Lack of cooperation between the two means of transportation meant that passengers had to get off the car from the center, walk across the tracks, and get back on another streetcar to go on to East Bridgewater. This was a horse-drawn operation for many years between the center of town and the tracks.

Following the close of ice-cream stands in the center of town due to increased traffic, a small stand was opened on Bedford Street at Legion Field, just opposite Worcester Street, in the 1940s. Producer's Dairy was easily accessible to the ever-increasing motorist population.

Four

SCHOOLS

The second building of the Bridgewater Academy, shown here in 1860, was built just in front of the current academy building in 1825. The first one, identical to this one and constructed in 1799, was located at the opposite end of the common. The loss of the first building by fire in February 1822 may have been the catalyst to bring about the layout of the town common. The land for both buildings and the common was donated by Major Lazell.

Pictured here in 1880, the third Bridgewater Academy building was erected in the 1868. It was constructed behind the second building so that classes would not be interrupted during the year. This structure stands today as the rear portion of the existing academy building.

This pictures was taken sometime after 1885, after the construction of the Memorial Building. Bridgewater Academy at one time supplied 25 percent of the students at Harvard University.

The fourth and final major addition to the Bridgewater Academy occurred in 1875, when a large section of four classrooms was added to the front of the building. The town took over the use of the building as a high school around this time. This photograph shows the structure in 1920. Following the opening of Bridgewater High School in 1951, the academy building was used for various town offices and the children's library. The building underwent a major renovation in 1968 to house the newly expanded police station.

Constructed in 1853, Schoolhouse No. 1, seen here in 1880, may have been moved to this location on the corner of Grove and Summer Streets. During an expansion of the college in 1890, it was closed when the new Normal Hall was built and took in many of the town's elementary students who lived near the center. The building was moved by A.J. Elwell to the town center, next to the hotel, to be used for commercial purposes.

The Dyer School was one of the many one-room schoolhouses in town located on the right at the beginning of Old Pleasant Street. These buildings, owned by the town, were often moved to different locations to service the needs of growing neighborhoods. This one was closed *c.* 1940 and was destroyed by fire in the 1960s.

Located at 288 High Street, the Prospect School provided education for the children of the Irish and Italian families employed by the ironworks. These small, wooden schools were often referred to as the "anything" schools. This one was also closed in the 1940s.

The Great Woods (or District No. 12) School was erected in 1876 to serve the families of the attendants of the Bridgewater State Workhouse, formerly called the Bridgewater State Almshouse. In 1882, Hollis M. Blackstone became the superintendent of the workhouse and continued to head the institution after it was renamed the Bridgewater State Farm in the late 1880s. Early in his 40-year tenure, the school was renamed in his honor. The Blackstone School stayed open until the early 1940s, making it one of the last outlying schools to close. It was located on the corner of Administration Road and Titicut Street.

The building of the William H. McElwain Grammar School from 1911 to 1913 was a major turning point in the history of the Bridgewater public school system. Fortunately for the town, J. Franklin McElwain donated money for a building lot on Main Street in honor of his deceased brother, William H., who had founded an important shoe firm in Bridgewater and shown a commitment to the civic welfare of the town. By 1914, the McElwain School had 292 pupils, making it the largest of the town-run public schools. This structure was used as a school until the 1990s, when a new elementary school was erected to serve most of Bridgewater's children. Although 90 years old, the McElwain building is still used for educational purposes.

Following the completion of the McElwain School, the town erected its first junior high school in 1918—the School Street School. In 1949, it was turned into an elementary school. It was later named the William Hunt School and was eventually sold to the college.

The first Bridgewater High School building, shown here between 1950 and 1960, was constructed by the town to replace the older academy building. Due to the rapid growth of the town, it was quickly replaced with the new regional high school in 1960 and was later used as a junior high for grades five through eight.

Five

FAIRGROUNDS, PARKS, AND FUN

The main entrance for the Plymouth County Agricultural Society fairgrounds stood on Broad Street in the general area of Brick Kiln Lane and Broad Street.

Shown here are the judging stand, grandstand, and cattle exhibition hall at the Plymouth County Agricultural Society fairgrounds. The grounds, extending from the Town River to High Street on the east side of Broad Street, consisted of over 60 acres along the river, purchased in 1855.

While the fair opened in 1819, displays were held on the lawn of the Academy or upper hall of Town Hall until 1851, when the property on Broad Street was developed as a fair grounds. This fair ran until c. 1900 as the largest agricultural fair in Plymouth County. In this view from Broad Street, the cattle barn, grandstand, and exhibition hall can be seen, along with the half-mile racetrack in the foreground. A shift from agriculture to manufacturing in the area led to the close of the grounds.

The main exhibition hall for the Plymouth County Agricultural Society fairgrounds was built in 1856 and held almost 3,000 people. It was also the largest function hall in town, serving many other events. It was destroyed by fire in 1890 and was replaced with a similar but less ornate building.

The second exhibition hall at the fairgrounds, built in 1891, was located on the east side of Broad Street just north of the Town River, about 100 yards off the road. Following the close of the fair in the late 1890s, J. Gardner Bassett purchased it and began the brick operation on the fairgrounds property in 1901. Bassett converted the exhibition hall to a shoe factory for the May's Slipper Company in 1908. It was torn down during World War II.

Pictured here *c.* 1880 is the Plymouth County Agricultural Society fair in operation, as seen from the upper floor of the exhibition hall. Following the close of the fair *c.* 1900, the property was used as the Bridgewater Brick Company until just after World War II. This operation left three ponds and a devastated landscape that reverted back to woodland. The town acquired the property in 1999, with state funds, for parkland.

The Plymouth County Agricultural Society began a joint exhibition with the Bridgewater Grange in 1913. The Grange Park fairgrounds were located in the general area of Grange Court, off South Street. The fair ran from 1913 to 1935. The exhibition hall and dining hall are now part of the Wood residence at 615 South Street.

This panoramic view of Grange Park shows the cattle barn, dining hall, and exhibition hall. The horse racetrack was also used for automobile racing.

Pilgrim Park was one of two dance halls built along the shore of Lake Nip in the Scotland section of town in the late 1800s. The two parks were also located on the trolley line to Taunton, making them very easy to get to for evening entertainment. Supposedly, because of the seedy reputation of these businesses, people departing from the Taunton-bound trolleys were quick to point out that they had only been shopping in the city of Taunton and would never stop at the "dance hall." Pilgrim Park was destroyed by fire in the 1920s.

The north side of the common is decorated for the Fourth of July parade in 1912. The three-story shop between the Odd Fellows building and the Redmen's hall is said to have had a glass wall on the rear of the third floor for a photography studio.

Each Fourth of July, O.B. Cole rolled out a small building next to his shop at the head of Summer Street, well stocked with a wide selection of fireworks for the holiday. This was obviously done to avoid losing his whole business should an accident occur.

The crowded square awaits the Fourth of July parade c. 1920. The Estes Block is decked out with the name "Bridgewater" spelled out on its second-floor window awning. R.J. Casey's store was founded in 1897. In the 1940s, his son Bart moved one more store over to sell newspapers, candy, cigarettes, and magazines as the Bridgewater News. A live radio broadcast of the Virginia Block fire in December 1924 was done from the radio studio on the second floor.

Following the end of World War I in 1918, a large victory parade was held in the town center. Here, two men inspect an army tank driven through town as part of the parade.

Whitman's pumper truck passes through Bridgewater in front of the Estes Block on parade day in 1947. The police stand can be seen in the lower right corner. Before the advent of traffic signals, a police officer stood in the square to direct traffic. Route 28 through the square was the main road to Cape Cod, over which thousands of cars passed on summer weekends.

The 1947 parade comes up School Street past the fire station. The original brick structure was painted white to match the additions and the fire tower. The building to the right of the station was a lodging house that was taken down in the early 1950s to make room for expansion of the station.

Horse Team No. 1 from McNeely's pulls the town's ancient steam pumper through the square on the Fourth of July in 1947. The home between the Estes Block and the Trust Company is that of Artemus Hale, built in the early 1800s. It was almost the site of the Memorial Reading Room in 1880.

Following the close of Grange Park, a small fairground called Flynn's Field was used on Main Street in the area of Old Forge Road from the late 1930s into the 1940s.

Townspeople prepare for the Fourth of July fair at Flynn's Field on Main Street *c.* 1948.

The Bridgewater Academy Marching Band, seen *c.* 1947, passes by the home of the Bridgewater Fire Department. While the academy was run by the town, students and teachers took great pride in continuing the name of the once famous private institution. It was not until 1952 that the name of Bridgewater High School was commonly used.

Coach Lester Lane poses on the front lawn of the academy with the 1929 baseball team. From left to right are the following: (front row) John Sweeny, Joe Stallon, Phi Calony, ? Hodgson, and Donald Burrill; (middle row) Art Carroll, Bruno Goviavoni, Chic Lancalis, Joe Vallon, Bob Baker, and Bill Halleon; (back row) Joe Joyce, Arthur Joyce, Martin Bodwicz, coach Lester Lane, Peco Palitroni, and Arthur Case.

Sports were even a big part of church life in town. Included in this *c.* 1915 view of the St. Thomas baseball team are Frank Cashon, John Dowd, Father Faralley, and William Bois.

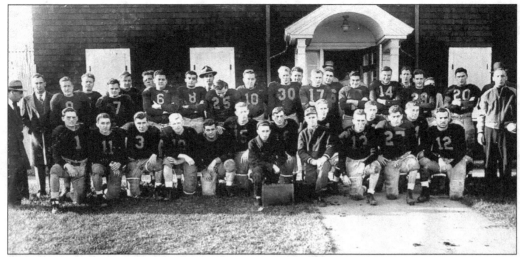

Prior to World War II, many of the area towns had a football team, including Bridgewater. These games were known to be much tougher than the high school matches and had a large following. Some of those shown here include coach Manny Souza, left guard Cookie "Lujack" Mahtesian (No. 12), right guard Eddie "Deadeye" Bonfiglioli (No. 24), left halfback John "Greyhound" Roderick (No. 27), right guard Dick Dowd, quarterback Moon Lazzaro (No. 13), and trainer Eddie Cripps.

The St. Thomas baseball team poses for a photograph. The batboy sits in front of the group. The others are, from left to right, as follows: (front row) F. Cashon, two unidentified players, the coach, Inky Kilbridge, and John Dowd; (back row) Tom Kilbridge, William Bois, ? Dunn, and three unidentified players.

Six

CENTRAL SQUARE

Central Square, as seen from Broad Street looking south, appeared like this prior to 1823. The first Bridgewater Academy can be seen to the left, and the fence is about where Stetson Street is today.

On the left of this photograph is the original Washburn farmhouse, built *c.* 1785 and taken down *c.* 1890. The store on the left was built by the Washburns and may have been used for a short time by Artemus Hale. Before becoming the famous Cole's Drug Store, it was used for many years by the Carver Washburn Company for the sale of cotton gins.

Mr. Eddy built this store in 1806 at the corner of Broad and Summer Streets. Originally a one-story building, a second floor was added later. The building was moved back 10-15 feet and then further modernized until it was demolished in 1910. Hale, Cole, Cholerton and others were associated with the store across the street on the other corner of Summer Street. Artemus Hale lived next door to this structure.

This photograph shows the lower common *c.* 1880, shaded with beautiful buttonwood trees. The Artemus Hale home was built by Edward Mitchell *c.* 1800 on the former Washburn farm grant. In the foreground is the town water pump and the public hay scale. The vast area in front of the pump was the original site of the Bridgewater Academy.

From the 1770s to the 1920s, many generations in Bridgewater came to rely on the variety and quality of the goods sold at Hooper and Clark (pictured in 1880). The building was located on the northwest corner of Central Square on what is now the Bridgewater Savings Bank parking lot. For over a century before Avery F. Hooper and P.O. Clark established their business in 1874, Col. Josiah Edson, who remained loyal to England during the American Revolution, maintained at this location what is considered to be the first store in Bridgewater. Around the close of the war, Isaac and Nathan Lazell went into business on the same site, erecting a new building in 1798. This store became associated with the Bridgewater Iron Company. It was enlarged several times and was carried on by various proprietors until it was taken over by Hooper and Clark. In its day, you could buy almost any item imaginable from thread to groceries to building materials.

This c. 1900 view shows the interior of the Hooper and Clark store. General stores served many needs of the community and sold anything from a packet of buttons to a wagonload of brick to build a home. This one served as a lending institution before banks and as a company store for the ironworks. Due to the great amount of business traffic from other towns, it was also the best source of news and a cup of grog for the weary traveler.

This painting was created *c.* 1900 and today hangs in the Bridgewater Public Library. It was used as the cover for Louise Dickinson Rich's book *Innocence under the Elms.* Louise Dickinson Rich came to Bridgewater in 1905 when her father took over the *Bridgewater Independent.* The book reflects her life as a young girl growing up in Bridgewater.

The second-oldest store in Bridgewater, Crane and Burrill was located on the corner of Broad and Summer Streets. It was built *c.* 1804, with a second floor added in 1825. Joshua E. Crane's association with this general country store began in 1844, when he came to Bridgewater to help his uncle Morton Eddy operate the business. In 1848, Crane became the sole proprietor, and for the next 40 years, this native of nearby Berkley became a beloved citizen, merchant, and historian of his adopted town. After his death in 1888, his son Henry L. ran the business in partnership with Henry T. Burrill. The partnership ended in 1902, when Crane decided to devote all his time to his work as Bridgewater's clerk and treasurer. The business continued as H.T. Burrill's and, in 1910, moved into a new building, which replaced the old 1804 structure. Today, the site is part of a parking lot serving a number of businesses.

Burrills Store — P.P. Dorr worked here

Pictured here is the head of Broad Street *c.* 1900, just before the demolition of the Burrill store. The store had been moved backwards (15 feet from its original location) to make room for the widening of the square in the mid-1800s.

A portion of this building was brought to Bridgewater by Abram Washburn from East Bridgewater center, in his attempt to develop Bridgewater center, after donating land for the town common. Over the years, the Bridgewater Inn grew in size and popularity to become a landmark in the area. It was well known for its fine food, lodging, and spring-mounted dance area on the second floor. The enterprise, also known as the Hyland House, was torn down in the 1930s.

Early drugstores, such as O.B. Cole's, were called apothecaries. Soda, or tonic, originally sold for medicinal purposes in apothecaries, led to the creation of soda fountains and ice-cream sales in these establishments. They soon became places to spend leisure time for young people, automobile travelers, and normal-school students. The Bridgewater Boston Express Company was formally owned by the Shed Company and specialized in delivering goods around town that were brought in by the train. By 1879, the establishment was owned by Mr. Bowman and Mr. Perkins.

This building, erected *c.* 1820 on land owned by the Washburn family, may have first been used as a store by Artemus Hale. It was most famous in the 1800s as the company store for the Carver Washburn Company and later the Carver Cotton Gin Company. O.B. Cole took over the property and ran a drugstore for many years, which later became Federal Drug and then Rexalls. In the mid-1900s, the main business in the building was Daiker's Flowers before it was taken over by Sam Cholerton's Insurance. In the 1980s, Estabrook and Chamberlain Insurance undertook an extensive renovation of the property.

Following the demise of O.B. Cole's, the store was taken over by Harold Mann, who joined the chain of Federal Drug. Seen here *c.* 1930 are, from left to right, his daughter Dorothy, Ed Lord, and Harold Mann.

This home stood at the head of Summer Street just south of the Bridgewater Trust Company. It was built in the late 1880s by O.B. Cole, who was also the proprietor of the drugstore across the street. The Cole house was taken down for the construction of a parking lot and the expansion of the bank in the early 1970s. The location was also that of the original Washburn home.

The town fountain was located in the general area of the old town pump, which once provided water for teams of horses and weary travelers passing through the square. This spot is where Summer Street leaves the square on the "Little Common." After falling into disrepair, the town fountain was taken away in a World War II scrap iron drive.

This splendid view depicts the Bridgewater Inn shortly before its demolition in the 1930s to make room for a gas station. To the left can be seen the Unitarian church steeple.

A streetcar passes through the square *c.* 1910, headed for Brockton. The electric streetcar company had two large facilities in town. A coal-fired power-generating station was located on the corner of Swift Avenue and Pleasant Street, and the carbarn was situated on the east side of Main Street at the West Bridgewater town line.

The former general store has been converted into a grocery store with the Dudley drugstore on the end, seen here in 1925, just prior to its demolition.

The Virginia Block, constructed *c.* 1910, stood on the corner of Main and Broad Streets. Retail shops occupied the first floor, professional offices the second, and apartments the third. There was also a waiting room on the first floor for passengers of the electric street railway. The building was destroyed by fire in January 1924.

A small but devastating fire struck the old general store on the corner of Main Street and Central Square *c.* 1920. The landmark, which had stood for more than 125 years, was damaged beyond repair and was eventually torn down to make way for a more modern J.J. Newberry's and a small drugstore. This picture was taken from one of the third-floor apartments in the Virginia Block, which would also be destroyed by fire a few years later.

Less than 25 years old, the Virginia Block was lost to fire one January evening. Patrolmen noticed the fire and were able to alert all of the tenants on the third floor. To the left can be seen Bassett's Ford Garage. In the right foreground is the town's first traffic signal, a flashing yellow light referred to as "the dummy." The current building on this site was built new from the foundation up.

The Estes Block stood on the corner of Broad and Summer Streets following the demolition of the Crane store. Casey's was the largest soda shop in town after the demise of O.B. Cole's across the street. Also in the building were the Brockton Edison Store and the Brockton Public Market. After the passing of Mr. Casey, his son Bart moved to a smaller storefront one door down and ran a popular newspaper and cigar concern until the early 1960s, when the block was torn down to make way for the new A&P.

Originally built as the Bridgewater Trust Company in the 1915, the Plymouth Home National Bank is pictured here in 1955. In the 1970s, the second floor was removed, the roofline was changed, and an addition was placed to the left of the building. The original name of the bank can still be seen on the door of the vault.

The Estes Block is seen here *c.* 1950. Following the downsizing of Casey's Ice Cream Parlor by son Bart Casey, the corner storefront was never successfully occupied again. The Republican Town Committee used the corner store for a local headquarters for the Nixon campaign in 1960, another failed venture.

J.J. Newberry's dominated Central Square when this photograph was taken in 1950. It filled the transition between the general store and the shopping center until it was torn down in the 1970s for the Bridgewater Savings Bank expansion.

Seven

ON AND ABOUT
THE COMMON

Following the separation of the populace into various churches in the 1820s, Bridgewater felt
the need to build its own town hall in the 1830s on the corner of School and Bedford Streets.
This artist's conception has appeared in many college publications over the years because the
town hall was used as the first location of the college from 1840 to 1846.

This view of the first town hall, as seen from the steeple of the Congregational church, differs from the college drawing because the building actually has four columns, not six. After the completion of the new town hall in 1843 and the erection of the new college building in 1846, the building was sold, moved to 31 Cedar Street, and converted to a home. The New Jerusalem Church was then built on this site in 1871.

The Bridgewater Town Hall is seen here c. 1880 with the town's new firehouse behind it. Horses that were used to pull the fire apparatus were also used by the highway crew while working on the streets. Tradition has it that when the alarm sounded, the horses were trained to run back to the station to harness up to the pumper.

This view of the west side of the common looks south *c. 1880*. The town watering trough, pump, and hay scales appear in the foreground. In the back, Crocker's Store, before the addition of the third floor and gambrel roof, can be seen.

Shown here is the common in 1910. On the left is the Bridgewater Inn. The next two-story building is the former Schoolhouse No. 1, which was moved from the corner of Grove and Summer in 1891. It was first known as the Elwell Block and later the Bowman Block. Next is the Mitchell Block, home to Haye's Ice Cream Parlor in 1902 and Ferguson's Shoe Store in 1879. Tradition says that when the land was donated in the 1830s by the Lazell family, it was originally laid out to the dimensions of Noah's Arc.

The Bridgewater Town Hall was built in 1843 to replace the smaller one across School Street. The second floor was used for many activities over the years, as sort of an "incubator" for businesses and churches that came to town. The first silent films were shown in the hall before the construction of the Princess Theater in the 1913. The town's first police station was located on the first floor along with other town offices. The town jail, consisting of four brick cells and a coal stove, was built in the 1870s on a small parcel behind Fairbank's and used until the early 1950s. The second floor was broken up into offices in the 1970s as the government grew. Cries for the building's replacement go back as far as 1900 due to its small size.

CENTRAL SQUARE, THE BAND STAND AND BRIDGWATER INN, BRIDGWATER, MASS.

The bandstand on the common was used by the town band for concerts on summer evenings before World War II. The last bandstand was built in 1901, replacing one that was about 30 years old. The decline of the band and increased traffic in the square brought an end to these events. In the 1950s, summer concerts were once again held on the college campus.

Schoolhouse No. 1 was originally built on the corner of Grove and Summer Streets. It was one of the first large school buildings to replace the many one-room schoolhouses around town. As was the custom of the day, buildings were moved to new locations rather than demolished. This structure was known as the Elwell, or Bowman, Block for many years after its relocation to the east side of the common.

The west side of the common c. 1910 had a trolley turnout in front of the Tory House. This was needed for loading passengers while other cars passed through in the opposite direction. The restaurant next to the Tory House was known as the Exchange Café.

In 1864, John H. Fairbanks erected this building next to the town hall. At that time, half of the building was occupied by William Prophett, first as a variety store and later as a furniture, home furnishing, and undertaking store. Up until the 1920s, there was a large furniture display case on the sidewalk in front of the store. Hyman Gotschalk took over the furniture business from Prophett and Flynn before moving it to Broad Street. The Fairbanks building was the first to be erected on this side of the common after the inn and the town hall.

This view looks across the common at the east side just after the relocation of Schoolhouse No. 1 and the construction of the Mitchell Block. The massive 100-foot town flagpole casts its shadow across the common in the afternoon sun.

The Fellowship Lodge, chartered in 1797 by Paul Revere, purchased this two-story building in 1840. In 1860, a second floor was added, and *c.* 1900 the front of the building was extended out to the street to make more room for the businesses on the first floor. Shown here in 1935, the building was torn down in 1967 to allow for the new Masonic lodge.

At the north end of the common was the Artemus Hale homestead. Hale offered this site for the Memorial Library, but it was turned down in favor of its current location on South Street. The great width of the sidewalk in front of the stores can be seen here, before it was reduced to accommodate diagonal parking spaces.

This *c.* 1920 photograph of the Bridgewater Town Hall shows the fire watchtower at the rear. The 20 feet of lawn and the granite fence in front of the building are now gone, making way for parking.

This *c.* 1880 view, looking across the head of School Street, shows the town hall. The firehouse can be seen at its rear. The ramp and wide passageway under the rear of the town hall was the storage area for the early highway department.

Shown here is the west side of the common *c.* 1890. Before the common, this was the only street running north–south through the center. The land for the common was donated by the Washburn family after the fire at the original Bridgewater Academy in 1823. Major Lazell also donated land for the Common at its southern end as he owned the "Tory" house at the time. He was also repsponsible for the layout of Bedford Street.

The south end of the common appeared such *c.* 1880. Note the width of the walk and lawn in front of the town hall. The massive flagpole that once stood on the end of the common can be seen.

Inhabiting the common in 1870 are, from left to right, the Masonic building; the Crocker home, which was moved to the rear and the barn brought forward *c.* 1910 to serve as a store; and Crocker's Store.

For 20 years, Robert Ferguson worked in the Bridgewater Iron Works, where his father, James Ferguson, was the superintendent. In 1879, the young Ferguson decided to open up a shoe store, first located on Main Street and later on the east side of Central Square. When he passed away in 1909, his son, Robert H. Ferguson, took over this flourishing business, which, by this time in 1910, had a shoe-repairing department. Robert was already well known in Bridgewater and surrounding communities as a solo cornetist and leader of the Bridgewater Band. Following in his father's footsteps, he played an active role in the civic life of the town.

The Servicemen's Canteen, shown here in 1944, was set up on the front lawn of the Bridgewater Academy during World War II. It served free meals and offered any needed assistance to servicemen passing through town. The structure was later moved to Cottage Street to serve the Bridgewater Visiting Nurse, scouting, and town recreation committees.

This print of the westerly side of the square in 1940 shows, from left to right, Stengal's Variety and Delicatessen, the Odd Fellows building, Thompson's Nationwide Groceries, the Redmen's building containing the post office, A&P, and J.J. Newberry's. On the far right is the Estes Block with Casey's Ice Cream Parlor on the left side and Brockton Edison on the right.

Central Square is pictured here in 1960. Before the opening of Route 24 in 1956, the town center was one of the main roads to Cape Cod. Thousands of automobiles passed through town, creating gridlock on summer Sunday afternoons. This situation occurred before the electric streetcars ended in 1927.

Eight

OFF THE COMMON

This c. 1870 photograph depicts Broad Street prior to electrification, with utility poles and streetcar tracks. The Gilbert estate can be seen behind the fence on the left. On the right, there are no structures from the J.B. Rogers tin shop down to the home of J.E. Winslow, at 53 Broad Street.

Broad Street appears here in 1880, before the elm trees fully matured to provide a natural canopy for the roadway. The numerous small retail shops lining the right side of the road opposite the Gilbert estate on the hill across the street included the Rogers tin shop, the first shop on the right while heading north on Broad. This photograph was taken just prior to the construction of the town's first and only movie theater, which eventually sat where the tree with the diagonal stripes is shown.

Broad Street is lined with beautiful elm trees c. 1900. The Gilbert estate can be seen on the rise on the left before the construction of the Virginia Block on its front lawn.

On Broad Street *c.* 1900, a natural tunnel was formed by the bows of the towering elm trees. The J.B. Rogers tin shop, the second building down on the left, was the source of the numerous tin roofs in town and the homes built in the late 1880s.

This *c.* 1920 view, looking toward the square, shows Broad Street. Maurice Gotshock's clothing store can be seen on the left just before the Princess Theater. The remains of the rise on the right are the front lawn of the Gilbert estate. This area was later leveled, and a diner car was placed there before the building of another gasoline station in the 1950s.

This view spans School Street across the south end of the common *c.* 1900. The New Jerusalem Church can be seen on the right. School Street drew its name from the town- and state-operated schools located there over the years.

The Bridgewater Memorial Library, on South Street, was erected in 1881 and was dedicated on Memorial Day 1882. It was built not only to serve as a public library for an expanding population but also as a town museum and Civil War memorial to honor the 36 young men of the town who gave their lives to end slavery and preserve the Union. Their names are inscribed on the Tennessee marble tablets at the entrance of the building. This structure was built with public funds and the contributions of the town's citizens rather than with money donated by a single wealthy patron.

Under the direction of Hollis M. Blackstone, the Bridgewater State Workhouse continued to expand and eventually evolve into a place of confinement along with the farm operation. This photograph shows the site *c.* 1900. This building would serve the needs of the state for almost 100 years until it closed around the year 2000. One of its most famous residents was "the Boston Strangler," Albert DeSalvo.

Looking south down Broad Street from High Street toward town *c.* 1880, one could see the massive fairground exhibition hall.

The storefronts along Broad Street at the railroad crossing appeared such *c.* 1880. The home is now gone, but both of the other buildings are still in use today.

This picture was taken from the spire of the Unitarian church, providing a view over the first normal-school building toward Summer Street *c.* 1850. Carver's Pond can be seen on the horizon over an almost treeless landscape, typical of the period.

Nine

HOMES ABOUT TOWN

This late-Federal-style house, built by Col. Abram Washburn, was built in 1825 and once stood at 9 Summer Street. It was located across the street from the original Washburn home on the original king's grant. In the 1930s, it was divided into apartments and finally torn down in 2001.

Snow Lodge was one of two identical homes that stood side by side at the beginning of Union Street just off Main Street. The first one was used as a restaurant and lodging house in the 1950s and 1960s before being destroyed by fire in the late 1970s.

Rev. John Shaw, who succeeded Rev. Benjamin Allen, the first minister of the First Parish, was the pastor for 60 years (1731–1791). Beginning in 1740, he used his newly built house at 15 Plymouth Street as a school to prepare boys and young men for college, especially Harvard and Brown. As late as 1884, Joshua Crane wrote that the Shaw house "has been the home of five generations, and is still in good repair. It should be preserved as a memorial of its honored builder." This was not to be. The Shaw homestead was torn down in 1904 to make way for Walter and Flora Little's new home.

The rear view of the Rev. John Shaw home shows a small shedlike structure, supposedly the remains of Colonel Edson's first general store, which was moved to this location *c.* 1775, when his new store was built in the square.

Walter and Flora Little built this beautiful home at 15 Plymouth Street c. 1908 on the site of the Shaw homestead. It was just up the street from the Eastern Grain Company, owned by Little. In later years, Flora Little donated generously to the Bridgewater Improvement Association and the town library. These funds have a large part in maintaining the beauty of our town center and the building of our new library. The brick home next door was built for Walter Little's father.

The Pratt Tavern stood for more than 120 years at the intersection of Pleasant Street and the corner of Swift Avenue at the present location of the Veterans of Foreign Wars hall and the former street railway power plant. The name is attributed to Asa Pratt, the first proprietor of the Bridgewater Inn. It served for many years as a way station for weary travelers before being disassembled in the early 1900s. After being purchased by the street railway, the building was used to house Italian laborers working on the track laying in 1897.

The A.H. Ward estate encompassed a portion of land on the south side of Park Terrace along Summer Street almost to Park Avenue. The land to the north side of the street was later developed into what was known for many years as the Bridgewater Normal School campus, or Boyden Park. The home was destroyed by fire just after 1900, and Park Terrace was laid out.

The Arthur Boyden home stood on the corner of Park Avenue and Summer Street across from the first cemetery. It was also situated across the street from the college campus park, which was later named in honor of Boyden and his son. The home was torn down in the late 1950s by the college to build a dormitory.

This massive home, the Hayward estate, once stood on the corner of Church and South Streets. It was taken down in the 1950s to make way for the Bridgewater Cooperative Bank and the telephone exchange.

This extensive farm, located at 350 Plymouth Street, was originally built for the Bassett family after 1730. About 100 years later, it was owned by Mitchell Hooper, who began a brick-making business along with the dairy farm. The dairy business ran for many years under the name of the Dutchland Farm and today is the site of the Waterford Village apartment complex.

The Hooper homestead was located on the corner of Grove and South Streets. The Hooper family is known in Bridgewater for the brickyards and general store in the center of town in the 1800s. The house was demolished in the 1920s to make way for the present home.

In 1885, Henry Prophett built this beautiful home at 107 Bedford Street. Prophett was a very successful real estate developer and builder of many fine homes in Bridgewater during the late 19th century. One of his trademarks was the extensive use of galvanized steel shingles, or "tin" roofs, which have successfully lasted more than 100 years.

The Sawyer home, at 28 School Street, as seen from 21 School Street. Dr. Sawyer had this home built c. 1830.

The Dea. Joseph Alden house, located on High Street near Sprague's Hill, is most likely the oldest house still extant in present-day Bridgewater. While there is some uncertainty about the date of its construction, it merits more recognition as one of the town's most important historical landmarks. It was built in the late 1600s for Joseph Alden, the second son of the famous Pilgrims John and Priscilla Alden. Some historians believe that an earlier dwelling may have existed across High Street, which, in the 18th century, was called Prudence Street (Lane).

The Lowe home was located on the site of the present middle school on South Street. The farmland behind it was purchased in 1920 to build Legion Field. The home was demolished in 1949 to make way for the new school.

The Gilbert home occupied the lot at the corner of Main and Broad Streets, a location best known for the massive three-story Virginia Block, which was erected on the front lawn of this home in 1913. By 1950, it was completely surrounded by brick-and-concrete structures before it was torn down.

The Gates House currently stands at the corner of Grove and Cedar Streets and serves as the college admissions office. The home was originally constructed as a wedding gift for his daughter by Joseph Hyde. At that time, it was located where the college administration building is today and overlooked the quadrangle from its rear side. This lot is also referred to in early deeds as the windmill lot. Samuel P. Gates acquired the house when he was the executor of Hyde's Estate and moved to the corner to make way for the current building. The house was left to his daughter with the understanding that it eventually would be given to the college.

This Federal-style home was originally built on Pleasant Street and was later moved to its current location at 600 Pleasant Street. It was the home of Reverend Gay, one of the first ministers of the Scotland Trinitarian Congregational Church in 1823.

Located on Summer Street, this house was built by the Snell family between 1760 and 1780. The Snell family is associated with the first iron foundries at Carver's Pond and with education in town. The porches were added in the 1800s and removed in the 1960s.

Dating from the 1730s, the Copeland home, at 311 South Street, was one of the oldest in Bridgewater before its demolition in 1998. For many years, this heavily modified old New England cape was owned by the Copeland family.

Edward Mitchell built this home at 21 School Street *c.* 1830. Mitchell served as the proprietor of the Hyland House, or Bridgewater Inn, for many years. In the 1870s, the home was owned by Rev. Theodore Wright, pastor of the New Jerusalem Church. By the 1890s, it was inhabited by Joseph Bowman, owner of the local Bowman's Express. Bowman's son is responsible for many of the fine photographs of Bridgewater that were taken around the turn of the century.

This home, located at 30 Plymouth Street, was originally built on Spring Street as a home for Calvin Washburn *c.* 1820. In 1827, it was sold to Henry Holmes, who occupied it for nearly the remainder of the century.

Located on Main Street, this beautiful home was built *c.* 1820 for a descendant of Reverend Sanger, an early minister of the South Parish. Over the years, it has served as both a residence and also as the Birchwood Inn in the early 1900s. The barn at the rear served as the first home of the Bridgewater Players, a local amateur theater group, in the 1940s and 1950s.

In the early 1700s, Col. Solomon Fobes had this Federal-style home built at 1085 Pleasant Street. It was occupied by his family for more than 100 years and served as a landmark for travelers heading to the West.

In 1860, George Bassett built this home at 46 Main Street. Soon after, it was taken over by Ira Conant, who lived there for many years. Conant was a Boston merchant in the manufacture of gossamer rubber products and hoop skirts. The property was converted to a lodging house, the Iron Fence Inn, in the 1960s.

Dr. Abraham T. Lowe built this substantial home *c.* 1845 at the corner of Pleasant and South Streets. For many years, it was in the hands of the Lowe family and was later occupied by Lewis Lowe. In the early 1900s, it was the home of Dr. Warren and for a short time was used as the Cranberry Inn. Since the 1950s, it has served as the Bridgewater Nursing Home.

This complex was built around the early 1900s on the southern end of Sturtevant's, or Steadman's, Pond at the end of South Street when it was thought that fresh country air cured a variety of ills. The complex was later used as a youth camp by Judge Steadman and as a refuge for Mayor Curly. The main house stood until the 1970s. The pond is a colonial iron millpond dating from 1707.

This home was built on a small hill on Broad Street where the shopping center is today. It was the home of Eleazer Carver's son and overlooked to the south the new Carver manufacturing plant on Spring Street and to the north the Plymouth County fairgrounds.

The Tory House, the first home in the town center, was built in the early 1700s. It gets its name from the rapid departure of Col. Josiah Edson, who remained loyal to the Crown at the time of the American Revolution. Over the years, it has been owned by the Washburns, Lazells, and the town while being used as a residence and an inn.

The "Four-Legged Tree Farm" was one of the most famous landmarks in town for more than 150 years. Eleazer Carver built the home for his bride and planted the four elms in 1833 across the street from his first plant. The four trees were later chained together to form the arch and remained a landmark for travelers heading south to the Cape along Summer Street, until they were destroyed by Dutch elm disease in the 1950s.

The prison in Bridgewater began as a poor farm in the early 1800s. This massive structure was built iby the state in 1854 as a workhouse for the poor. At that time, it consisted of more than 800 acres on which the residents farmed, producing food for themselves and selling some at the market. This building burned in 1883.

Mass. State Farm. The Main Section
Bridgewater, Mass.

At the very time that Hollis M. Blackstone became the superintendent of the Bridgewater State Workhouse in 1883, a conflagration destroyed the wooden facility of the almshouse-workhouse, which dated from the 1850s. The process of rebuilding began almost immediately, following the detailed plans of Blackstone. Not surprisingly, it was decided that the new structures had to be fireproof, making it imperative to use brick, granite, and concrete instead of wood. In 1887, the fourth year of what would prove to be Blackstone's 40-year tenure as superintendent, the name of the institution was changed again. From 1887 to 1955, it was called the Bridgewater State Farm, and it was indeed once the biggest farm in Massachusetts. Today, we know it as the Massachusetts Correctional Institution.

Ten

POLICE AND FIRE

Taken *c.* 1870, this is probably the earliest photograph of the Bridgewater Fire Station. The lodging house was not yet built between it and the Hunt home on School Street.

After years of neglect and storage, volunteers restored Ousamequin No. 1 to its original beauty. Mel Gay (left), Buck Jordan (center), and Frank Goodrich prepare it for a parade *c.* 1947.

Steam pumps replaced the Ousamequin hand pumper in the 1880s. They were in turn replaced by gasoline-powered pumping trucks after 1910.

Members of the Bridgewater Fire Department pose outside the station in 1888. Horses were usually privately owned and had to be borrowed in order to pull equipment to a fire. The first alarm was the Congregational church bell.

The Bridgewater Fire Department hose wagon is on display in 1888. Water was pumped by steam from ponds, streams, or brick cisterns constructed around town. During the college fire of 1924, the Brockton pumper was destroyed because it sucked the campus pond dry and drew mud into the pump. Hydrants were first installed in 1887, replacing the few cisterns that were only in the town center and the head of Pleasant Street.

The Bridgewater Fire Department pumper and the chief's car sit at the corner of School and Cedar Streets in 1915. In the background can be seen the Gates House before it was moved to the corner of Cedar and Grove Streets to make room for the state college administration building.

This c. 1938 photograph of the Bridgewater Fire Department shows the expansion of the station to four bays with a fire tower.

The fire tower, built *c.* 1900, served as a watchtower for forest fires but also as a structure for drying hoses after a fire. During World War II, it was used as a spotting tower for civil defense groups monitoring the movement of aircraft over the town. It is shown here in 1946.

Call firemen line up at the foot of School Street *c.* 1942. The members of Bridgewater Auxiliary Fire Company A are, from left to right, as follows: (front row) Wilbur Greg, unidentified, Frank Burrill, and two unidentified men; (back row) Preston Balboni, Cliff Gerior, Arthur Rhodes, ? Waite (past chief), Joe Roque, Deputy Hector LeGard, and two unidentified men.

The members of the 1942 Bridgewater Auxiliary Fire Company B includes Wilbur Greg, John Dorr, Frank Burrill, George Austin, Preston Balboni, Cliff Gerior, Arthur Rhodes, former chief Waite, Joe Roque, Deputy Hector Legard, Warren Barnes and driver Brigham Basset.

Fire apparatus is lined up before coming up School Street for a parade c. 1947.

Policemen Chris O'Leary, Bob Hanlon, James Moore (chief), Tom Chestna, and Elmer Shaw are about to step off for another parade in 1948. Around the turn of the century, Bridgewater transitioned from a constable enforcing the law to a regular police department. A room was set up on the first floor of the town hall for use as a station. The lockup was a small four-cell building behind the hardware store, which was used until the early 1950s, when the station was moved to the academy building.

Chief James Moore convinced the town *c.* 1930 that his department needed a motorcycle to negotiate the Cape-bound traffic jams in the center of town on weekends. A bright-red 1930 Indian motorcycle was added to the force and remained in use for a few years until being damaged in an accident. More than 60 years later, the police department finally rode motorcycles again.

Bridgewater was a "dry" town from 1890 to the end of Prohibition. During that time, Chief Moore led a number of raids to put illegal stills out of business. The upper level of the town hall was used for evidence storage. A story tells that the chairman of the board of selectmen stopped by a particular home to pick up a bottle one evening, not realizing that the chief had raided the home the night before.

Shown here are the area chiefs of police on parade in the late 1920s. Many of these men were called to testify at the famous Sacco and Vanzetti trial because of robberies in the area.

Chief Jimmy Moore poses with Jeannette Mola, the local March of Dimes poster child *c.* 1950. Chief Moore was in office from 1922 to 1952, and one of his favorite jobs was working with children. He would often have troubled children sentenced to Sunday school rather than a sentence through the court system.

This photograph shows Police Chief Jimmy Moore and Fire Chief Frank Goodrich after a tough night on the job.

Eleven

THE COLLEGE

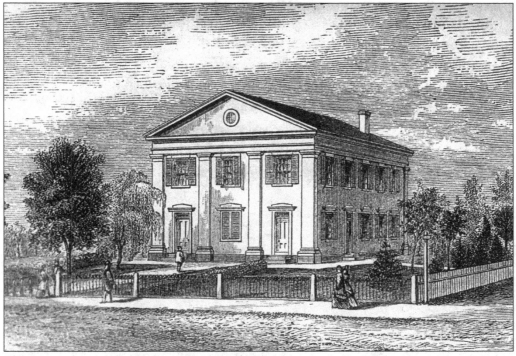

The first session of the Bridgewater Normal School began on September 9, 1840, meeting in temporary quarters in the old town hall on the southern corner of Bedford and School Streets. In 1845, the state legislature decided to erect buildings for the normal schools at Westfield and Bridgewater, an important step in establishing a permanent system for the training of teachers. The first state normal-school building in the United States, pictured here, was erected in Bridgewater in 1846 at the corner of Summer and School Streets on land donated by Abrams Washburn, one of the town's leading citizens. This plain, two-story wooden building was not a magnificent structure, but it was a promising start to a string of buildings that would grace an expanding campus in the years to come. While this structure is no longer extant, a small stone marker reminds passersby of the historic significance of this site.

The Bridgewater Normal School is shown here in 1871 after the addition of a third floor. In 1881, a third building was constructed as a detached science building at the rear of the hall and was known as the Cottage. In 1890, the Cottage building was moved to the corner of Grove and Summer Streets for use as a dormitory.

This 1875 photograph shows Normal Hall from the corner of School and Summer Streets. The center section was built in 1869, and two wings were added in 1873. It was the last large wooden structure built for the college.

Normal Hall is seen here from Grove Street *c.* 1875. The president of the college lived in the center section, and boys were on one side, girls on the other.

This photograph, taken from the front of the Unitarian church on School Street in 1891, depicts the college buildings. Originally built as two floors, the third floor was added in 1894, for the model or training school. A duplicate of this massive edifice can be seen at Framingham State College today. This building was used for less than 34 years before being destroyed by fire in 1924.

This photograph, taken *c.* 1900 from Grove Street, shows the rear of the normal school, Normal Hall, and a third building known as the Cottage. This structure was built in 1881 at the rear of the second normal school as a science annex. It was moved to this location for use as a dorm and destroyed in the 1924 college fire along with the new Normal Hall and the first Tillinghast Hall.

Shown here is the normal-school fire in 1924. Following the loss of the model school, various buildings around town were used to house students from the college. Kindergarten classes where held in the basement of the New Jerusalem Church at the head of School Street.

This photograph of children engaged in constructive work in the model-school classroom was the only one to survive the fire. It was found in a backyard a few blocks from the college.

The original Tillinghast Hall, seen here c. 1895, was built on the corner of Grove and Summer Streets as the first brick dormitory for the college. It was destroyed in the fire of 1924, and the name was given to the former Normal Hall replacement, which stood on the corner of School and Summer Streets.

After the Campus Pond was completed, an icehouse was erected to store ice for refrigeration in the warmer months of the year. Due to its highly visible location, it was one of the most attractive icehouses in the area. Its walls were about two feet thick and filled with sawdust for insulation.

Located in Boyden Hall, this auditorium served the town and college for many years as the largest hall in town. Town meetings were held here until the construction of Bridgewater Raynham Regional High.

124

The greenhouse in the college's botanical science garden was donated by Mrs. E.R. Steven for use in studying botany. This garden was a showplace at the head of Park Avenue for many years under the care of Prof. Louis Stearns.

View in Park, Bridgewater, Mass.

During the 1880s, the acquisition of more space became one of the priorities of the normal school, best illustrated by the addition of six acres of land on Summer Street across from the boarding hall. Initially, the state refused to purchase the land, prompting Principal Boyden to buy it in a private transaction. In 1886, the state did agree to buy it from Boyden, adding greatly to the size of the campus. This new area became known as Boyden Park and over the years became a great source of delight for the school and town, with its excavated pond, icehouse, tennis courts, croquet grounds, spaces for other sports, and beautiful setting graduation exercises. Much of this land is now taken up by the college's student union and a men's dormitory.

125

This *c.* 1890 photograph of Boyden Park was taken from the end of School Street heading southeast toward Park Avenue. The college purchased the land in 1883 for recreation. The lack of trees, characteristic of the town in this period, is very evident.

State Normal School, Bridgewater, Mass.

The beautiful pond in the center of Boyden Park, shown here in 1920, also served as the site for the annual tug-of-war between the classes at the school. The loser got a cool dip in the otherwise serene waters.

By the 1940s, the Boyden Park area was known by many of the neighbors as the campus. The pond had been filled and a tennis court had been constructed on the right side. The park also served the school as an athletic practice field before the construction of the new student union building in the 1960s.

Despite the tremendous expansion of Bridgewater State College in the last several decades, Boyden Hall, often called the administration building, remains an important centerpiece of the campus. Designed in the neo-Georgian tradition, this structure was erected after a disastrous fire destroyed three buildings of the Bridgewater Normal School on December 10, 1924. The land for this impressive building was bequeathed to the school by Samuel P. Gates, a banker, businessman, and civic-minded citizen of the town. Boyden Hall was named in honor of Albert Gardner Boyden and his son Arthur Clarke Boyden, principals of the normal school from 1860 to 1906 and 1906 to 1933, respectively. An inscription on a tablet inside the main door reads, "They gave their hearts, their minds, and their lives to this school." Over the years, changes have been made to the interior of the building, with a major renovation project taking place in the 1980s.

The current Woodward Hall was built in 1917 on Grove Street. Grove Street bordered a parcel of land donated to the college by two alumni, Dr. Lowe and Samuel Gates, in 1887.

The Albert Gardner Boyden Memorial Gymnasium was the last building erected at the Bridgewater Normal School during the long principalship of Boyden (1860–1906). Seeing the need for a new facility to accommodate the needs of a growing school, he began to advocate a new gymnasium in 1901, and in the following year, the state agreed to buy from the First Parish. Despite some initial opposition in the town, parish, and legislature, the project began in November 1903 on this beautiful piece of land that sloped gently down to Summer Street and Boyden Park beyond. Built at a cost of $60,000, this brick structure—with features associated with Queen Anne architecture—was dedicated on June 24, 1905, and was considered to be one of the finest gymnasiums in the state. It served the institution for more than 50 years in this capacity, before being converted into a library and then a building for the art department.